Copyright © 2023 David Richardson

All rights reserved. All rights reserved. No part of this guidebook may be reproduced by any mechanical, photographic, or electronic process, or in the form of a phonographic recording; nor may it be stored in a retrieval system, transmitted, or otherwise be copied for public or private use – other than for 'fair use' as brief quotations embodied in articles and reviews without prior written permission of the publisher and author. The intent of the author is only to offer their interpretation and information of a general nature to you on video production. In the event you use any of the information in this guidebook for yourself, the author and publisher assume no responsibility for your actions.

ISBN: 9798854186803

I would like to thank all my family, friends, and colleagues in guiding me on my journey over 25+ years in Wedding Video Production on writing my third book. I would also like to thank Andy Hall & Andy Preston for encouraging me in writing these books. Along with my Mastermind Group.

David Richardson, the author of this comprehensive wedding guidebook, brings with him a remarkable 30-year career during which he has skilfully filmed over 700 weddings. His vast experience and unwavering dedication make him an invaluable resource for couples seeking guidance in planning their special day.

As someone who has witnessed a wide array of scenarios, both moments of pure joy and unforeseen challenges, David understands that no matter how meticulously planned, unexpected situations can arise during weddings. Nevertheless, his extensive knowledge has not only allowed him to effortlessly navigate these situations but also enabled him to do so with professionalism and composure.

This guide is a testament to David's commitment to sharing his expertise and insights. Its purpose is to assist couples in navigating the complexities of wedding planning, ensuring a seamless and enjoyable experience. Drawing on his years of experience, David offers valuable tips on organization, time management, etiquette, and crisis management, providing readers with a comprehensive roadmap for each stage of wedding planning and the wedding day itself.

The underlying theme of remaining calm, flexible, and prepared for the unexpected is a reflection of David's understanding that even with careful planning, challenges can still arise. By empowering couples with knowledge and tools to proactively address potential obstacles gracefully, the guide allows them to fully immerse themselves in what truly matters: celebrating their love and beginning their married life together.

With a professional and polished tone throughout, this guide is a must-have resource for couples seeking a truly unforgettable wedding experience.

Chapter 1

Congratulations on beginning the exciting journey of wedding planning! Planning a wedding can be a wonderful and memorable experience, but it can also be a bit overwhelming. Here are some steps to help you get started on the right foot:

1. **Set a Budget: ** Determine how much you and your partner are willing to spend on the wedding. Creating a budget early on will help you make decisions throughout the planning process and ensure you do not overspend.

2. **Create a Timeline: ** Decide on a wedding date or a few possible dates. Having a timeline in mind will help you stay organized and book venues and vendors accordingly.

3. **Draft a Guest List: ** Start putting together a list of guests you want to invite. The number of guests will impact your venue choice and overall budget.

4. **Choose a Venue: ** Research and visit potential wedding venues. Consider factors like location, capacity, style, and amenities. Once you find the perfect venue, book it as soon as possible.

5. **Select Vendors:** Research and choose key vendors such as caterers, photographers, florists, and musicians. Read reviews, ask for recommendations, and meet with potential vendors to ensure they align with your vision.

6. **Design Your Theme and Style:** Decide on a theme or style for your wedding. This will guide your choices in terms of decor, colours, and overall ambiance.

7. **Send Save-the-Dates and Invitations:** Once you have your date and venue confirmed, send out save-the-date cards to give your guests a heads-up. Later, send formal invitations with all the necessary details.

8. **Plan the Ceremony and Reception:** Work with your partner and possibly a wedding planner to plan the flow of events during the ceremony and reception. Consider the order of events, music choices, and any special traditions you want to include.

9. **Organize Transportation and Accommodation:** If needed, arrange transportation for guests and book accommodations for those coming from out of town.

10. **Shop for Attire:** Start looking for your wedding attire, as well as outfits for the bridal party and groomsmen. Allow ample time for fittings and alterations.

11. **Arrange for Officiant and Marriage License:** If you haven't already, find an officiant who will conduct your wedding ceremony. Also, ensure you obtain the necessary marriage license.

12. **Plan the Honeymoon:** If you plan to go on a honeymoon after the wedding, start researching destinations and booking flights and accommodations.

13. **Organize Rehearsal Dinner:** If you choose to have a rehearsal dinner, make arrangements and send out invitations to those who will be attending.

14. **Finalize Details:** In the weeks leading up to the wedding, confirm all arrangements with vendors and the venue. Create a detailed timeline for the wedding day and share it with everyone involved.

15. **Enjoy Your Wedding Day: ** Finally, relax and enjoy your special day! Surround yourself with loved ones, and do not worry about the small details. Embrace the joy of the moment and celebrate the beginning of your new journey together.

Remember, wedding planning can be demanding, but it is essential to communicate openly with your partner and delegate tasks to family or friends when needed. Happy planning, and best wishes for a beautiful wedding!

Chapter 2: Defining Your Vision: Creating Your Dream Wedding

Once you have taken the initial steps of setting a budget, securing a venue, and choosing a date, it's time to dive into the heart of wedding planning: defining your vision for the dream wedding you've always imagined. This chapter will guide you through the process of creating a wedding that reflects your unique style and personality.

1. **Create a Vision Board:** Start by gathering inspiration from various sources like wedding magazines, Pinterest, or online wedding blogs. Create a vision board with images, colours, decor ideas, and themes that resonate with you. This will help you visualize the overall look and feel of your wedding.

2. **Decide on the Style:** Based on your vision board, identify the overall style you want for your wedding. It could be classic, rustic, bohemian, modern, vintage, or a combination of styles. Having a clear style in mind will guide your choices throughout the planning process.

3. **Choose Your Colours:** Select a colour palette that complements your chosen style and resonates with you as a

couple. Consider the season and the ambiance you want to create. Your colours will influence everything from decorations to attire.

4. **Personalize Your Wedding: ** Infuse your personalities and love story into the wedding elements. Consider incorporating personal touches, such as favourite quotes, shared hobbies, or cultural traditions.

5. **Set Priorities: ** Discuss with your partner and identify the aspects of the wedding that are most important to both of you. Whether it is the photography, food, music, or venue, knowing your priorities will help you allocate your budget wisely.

6. **Consider the Guest Experience: ** Think about your guests' experience from the moment they arrive at the venue until the last dance. Provide amenities like welcome bags, comfortable seating, and thoughtful Favors that will make your guests feel appreciated.

7. **Plan the Ceremony: ** Work with your partner and the officiant to create a meaningful and personalized ceremony. Include readings, vows, or rituals that hold significance for both of you.

8. **Design the Reception Space:** Work with your chosen venue or a decorator to bring your vision to life. Select centrepieces, table settings, lighting, and other decor elements that align with your chosen style and colours.

9. **Curate the Menu:** Collaborate with your caterer to design a menu that reflects your tastes and preferences. Consider any dietary restrictions or cultural food choices for a diverse dining experience.

10. **Entertainment and Music:** Book entertainment that matches your wedding style, whether it's a live band, a DJ, or a combination of both. Include songs that hold special meaning for you and your partner.

11. **Plan for Children and Pets:** If you expect children or pets to be part of the celebration, make arrangements to keep them comfortable and entertained during the event.

12. **Photography and Videography:** Choose a photographer and videographer whose work you love. These professionals will capture the precious moments of your wedding day, allowing you to relive them for years to come.

13. **Wedding Attire:** Make appointments for fittings and alterations for your wedding attire. Ensure that the outfits for the bridal party and groomsmen complement the overall style.

14. **Coordinate with Wedding Party:** Communicate with your wedding party, providing them with necessary details and schedules. Consider giving them thoughtful gifts as a token of appreciation.

15. **Embrace Flexibility:** While it's essential to have a vision, be open to adjustments and unexpected changes. Remember that some things might not go as planned, and that's okay. Embrace the spontaneity and enjoy the day regardless.

Defining your vision and creating your dream wedding should be a collaborative and enjoyable experience for you and your partner. Keep the lines of communication open, be true to yourselves, and let your love story shine through every aspect of your wedding. Happy planning!

Chapter 3: Setting a Solid Foundation: Budgeting and Financial Planning

Weddings can be a significant financial investment, so it's essential to set a solid foundation for budgeting and financial planning. This chapter will help you navigate the financial aspects of your wedding, ensuring that you stay within your means while creating the wedding of your dreams.

1. **Review Your Finances: ** Sit down with your partner and assess your current financial situation. Take a close look at your savings, income, and any outstanding debts. Understanding your financial standing will help you determine a realistic budget.

2. **Determine Your Total Budget: ** Decide on the total amount you are comfortable spending on your wedding. This amount may come from savings, contributions from family members, or a combination of both.

3. **Allocate Your Budget: ** Break down your total budget into categories such as venue, catering, attire, photography,

entertainment, and decorations. Allocate a specific amount to each category based on your priorities.

4. **Research and Get Quotes:** Research various vendors and venues to get an idea of their pricing. Contact them for quotes and ensure they fit within your allocated budget. Be prepared to negotiate and ask about package deals.

5. **Prioritize Your Expenses:** As you receive quotes, prioritize your expenses based on what matters most to you and your partner. Allocate more funds to your top priorities and be prepared to adjust in other areas.

6. **Create a Contingency Fund:** It's a good idea to set aside a contingency fund of about 5-10% of your total budget to account for unexpected expenses or last-minute changes.

7. **Track Your Spending:** Use spreadsheets or budgeting tools to track your spending throughout the planning process. This will help you stay organized and avoid overspending in any category.

8. **Consider DIY Options:** If you're crafty or have skilled friends or family members, consider DIY projects for some aspects of the wedding, such as decorations or Favours. This can help save money while adding a delicate touch.

9. **Guest List Management:** The number of guests directly impacts your catering and venue costs. Consider trimming the guest list if necessary to stay within your budget.

10. **Payment Schedule:** Understand the payment schedule for your vendors and plan accordingly. Some vendors may require a deposit upfront, while others may allow you to pay closer to the wedding date.

11. **Open Communication with Family:** If family members are contributing to the wedding budget, have open and honest conversations about the financial arrangements. Clarify expectations and ensure everyone is on the same page.

12. **Explore Financing Options:** If you need additional financial assistance, research financing options like personal loans or credit cards. However, be cautious and only borrow what you can comfortably repay.

13. **Review Contracts:** Before signing contracts with vendors, carefully review all terms and conditions to avoid any hidden costs or surprises.

14. **Regular Budget Check-Ins:** Throughout the planning process, have regular check-ins with your partner to review the budget and make adjustments as needed.

15. **Practice Gratitude:** Remember that a wedding is a celebration of love and commitment. Focus on the meaningful aspects of your special day rather than getting caught up in excessive spending.

By setting a well-planned budget and being mindful of your spending, you can ensure that your wedding is not only beautiful but also financially responsible. Working together with your partner and communicating openly about your financial goals will help you create a wedding that is both memorable and financially manageable.

Chapter 4: Finding the Perfect Venue: Location, Location, Location

Selecting the perfect wedding venue is one of the most crucial decisions you'll make during the planning process. The venue sets the tone for your wedding and impacts many other aspects of your big day. This chapter will guide you through the process of finding the ideal venue that suits your vision and budget.

1. **Determine Your Wedding Style:** Revisit the vision board and style you created in Chapter 2. The venue you choose should align with the overall theme and ambiance you want to create.

2. **Consider Your Guest List:** Have a rough estimate of the number of guests you plan to invite. Ensure that the venue can comfortably accommodate your guest count without being too cramped or overly spacious.

3. **Set a Location:** Decide on the general area or region where you want your wedding to take place. Consider both the convenience for your guests and the significance of the location to you and your partner.

4. **Research Venues:** Utilize online resources, wedding directories, and social media to research potential venues in your chosen location. Make a list of venues that catch your eye and fit within your budget.

5. **Visit Venues:** Schedule appointments to visit your shortlisted venues in person. Take a tour of the facilities and ask questions about what is included in the package.

6. **Venue Capacity and Layout:** Check the venue's maximum capacity and the layout of the space. Ensure there is enough room for your guests, as well as designated areas for the ceremony, cocktail hour, and reception.

7. **Consider Venue Restrictions:** Inquire about any restrictions or rules imposed by the venue, such as noise limits, decor guidelines, or end time restrictions.

8. **Outdoor vs. Indoor:** Decide whether you want an indoor or outdoor wedding, or a combination of both. Keep weather considerations in mind for outdoor venues and ensure there is a backup plan in case of inclement weather.

9. **Parking and Accessibility:** Check if the venue offers ample parking or if there are nearby parking options for your guests. Additionally, consider the accessibility of the venue for all guests, including those with mobility issues.

10. **Venue Amenities and Services:** Inquire about the amenities and services provided by the venue. Some venues may offer catering, decor, and audiovisual equipment, which could simplify your planning process.

11. **Costs and Packages:** Request detailed pricing information and packages from each venue. Compare the costs and what is included in each package to make an informed decision.

12. **Read Reviews and References:** Look for reviews and testimonials from other couples who have hosted their weddings at the venues you're considering. This can provide valuable insights into the venue's quality and service.

13. **Flexibility and Personalization:** Ask the venue if they allow personalization and customization of the space to make it uniquely yours.

14. **Venue Coordinator or Planner: ** Check if the venue provides an on-site coordinator or if you need to hire a wedding planner to manage the logistics on the day of the wedding.

15. **Trust Your Instincts: ** Above all, trust your instincts and go with the venue that feels right for you and your partner. Your gut feeling is often a good indicator of whether a venue will be the perfect fit for your dream wedding.

Once you've found the perfect venue, don't hesitate to book it promptly, as popular venues tend to fill up quickly. Choosing the right venue will set the stage for a magical and memorable wedding day for you, your partner, and your guests.

Chapter 5: Assembling Your Dream Team: Selecting Vendors and Professionals

Creating your dream wedding requires the expertise and talents of various vendors and professionals. Assembling the right team will ensure that every aspect of your wedding is executed flawlessly. This chapter will guide you through the process of selecting the perfect vendors to bring your vision to life.

1. **Prioritize Vendors:** Identify the key vendors you need based on your priorities and wedding style. Common vendors include a photographer, caterer, florist, videographer, wedding planner/coordinator, and entertainment (e.g., DJ or band).

2. **Do Your Research:** Begin researching potential vendors in your area. Utilize online platforms, read reviews, and ask for recommendations from friends, family, or other couples who recently got married.

3. **Check Portfolios and Previous Work:** Review the portfolios, galleries, or social media profiles of the vendors you're interested in. Assess their work to ensure it aligns with your style and preferences.

4. **Meet with Potential Vendors:** Schedule meetings or consultations with the vendors on your shortlist. This will allow you to discuss your vision, ask questions, and gauge their professionalism and expertise.

5. **Ask for References:** Request references from past clients to gain insights into their experiences working with the vendor. Happy clients are a good sign of a reliable vendor.

6. **Understand Pricing and Packages:** Inquire about pricing, packages, and any additional fees associated with the services. Be clear about what is included in each package and if there are any customization options.

7. **Compare and Negotiate:** Obtain quotes from multiple vendors in each category and compare their offerings. Don't be afraid to negotiate to get the best value within your budget.

8. **Consider Personality and Communication:** Choose vendors who are not only skilled professionals but also have great communication skills and a personality that meshes well with yours. You'll be working closely with them leading up to and on your wedding day.

9. **Review Contracts: ** Before finalizing any agreements, thoroughly read and understand the contracts. Ensure that all services, fees, and expectations are clearly outlined in writing.

10. **Book Early: ** Secure your preferred vendors as early as possible, especially for popular dates. Many top vendors get booked well in advance.

11. **Photographer and Videographer: ** These professionals will capture the memories of your special day. Choose ones whose style resonates with you and who can document your wedding day beautifully.

12. **Caterer: ** Sample the menu offerings from potential caterers and ensure they can accommodate any dietary preferences or restrictions for you and your guests.

13. **Florist: ** Look for a florist who can create stunning arrangements that match your colour scheme and wedding theme.

14. **Entertainment:** Book a DJ, live band, or other entertainment that can keep your guests dancing and having a great time.

15. **Wedding Planner/Coordinator:** If you haven't hired a wedding planner yet, consider doing so to assist with the logistics and coordination on your big day.

As you assemble your dream team of vendors, remember that clear communication, trust, and shared vision are essential elements for a successful collaboration. Working with a team of skilled and passionate professionals will ensure that your wedding day is everything you've ever dreamed of.

Chapter 6: Capturing Memories: Photography and Videography

Photography and videography are essential elements of your wedding day, as they capture the cherished memories that will last a lifetime. This chapter focuses on selecting the right photographers and videographers to document your special day in a way that reflects your unique love story.

1. **Start Early: ** Begin your search for photographers and videographers as soon as you have your wedding date and venue booked. Top professionals tend to get booked quickly, so securing them early is crucial.

2. **Define Your Style: ** Determine the style of photography and videography that resonates with you. Do you prefer traditional, candid, documentary, or artistic approaches? Consider the mood and emotions you want to convey through your visual memories.

3. **Browse Portfolios and Galleries: ** Review the portfolios and sample albums/videos of potential photographers and videographers. Look for consistency in their work and how well they capture emotions and details.

4. **Read Reviews and Testimonials:** Check online reviews and ask for references from past clients to learn about their experiences working with the photographer or videographer.

5. **Meet in Person or Virtually:** Schedule meetings or video calls with your top choices. Discuss your vision for the wedding, share your love story, and ensure you feel comfortable and confident with them.

6. **Ask About Experience and Equipment:** Inquire about their experience with weddings, the number of weddings they've shot, and the equipment they use. Experienced professionals are better prepared to handle different situations.

7. **Check for Compatibility:** Your photographer and videographer will be with you throughout your wedding day. Ensure that your personalities mesh well, as this will help you feel more relaxed and natural in front of the camera.

8. **Discuss Packages and Pricing:** Understand the packages they offer, including hours of coverage, the number of photos or video footage you'll receive, and any additional services or add-ons.

9. **Request a Sample Wedding:** If possible, ask to see a full wedding album or video from start to finish. This will give you a better idea of their storytelling skills and how they capture the entire day.

10. **Ask About Backup Plans:** Inquire about their contingency plans in case of equipment failure or unforeseen circumstances on the wedding day.

11. **Clear Image and Video Rights:** Discuss copyright and ownership of the photos and videos. Ensure that you have the right to share, print, and use them as you wish.

12. **Pre-Wedding Photoshoot or Engagement Video:** Consider booking a pre-wedding photoshoot or engagement video session. This will give you a chance to get to know your photographer and videographer better and get comfortable in front of the camera.

13. **Coordinate with Your Wedding Planner:** If you have a wedding planner, involve them in the discussions with your photographers and videographers to ensure a seamless flow of events on the day.

14. **Timeline and Shot List:** Collaborate with your photographers and videographers to create a timeline and shot list for the day. Share any specific moments or family members you want to be captured.

15. **Trust Your Team:** Once you've chosen your photographers and videographers, trust their expertise and artistic vision. Let them capture the magic of your wedding day while you enjoy every moment.

By selecting the right photographers and videographers who understand your love story and vision, you'll have beautiful and authentic visual memories to cherish for generations to come. Their artistry will enable you to relive the emotions and joy of your wedding day whenever you look back on the photographs and videos.

Chapter 7: Dress to Impress: Attire and Fashion for the Big Day

Choosing the perfect attire for your wedding day is an exciting and significant decision. This chapter will guide you through the process of finding the ideal wedding attire for both you and your wedding party, ensuring that everyone looks their best and feels confident on the big day.

1. **Start Early: ** Begin shopping for your wedding attire well in advance, especially if you plan on having a custom-made dress or suit. Allow ample time for fittings and alterations.

2. **Set a Budget: ** Determine how much you're willing to spend on your wedding attire, including accessories and shoes. Remember to consider the attire for your wedding party if you're covering the cost.

3. **Bridal Gown and Accessories: ** Start shopping for your bridal gown, considering the style that complements your body shape and reflects your personality. Don't forget to shop for accessories such as veil, jewellery, and shoes.

4. **Groom's Attire: ** Select the groom's suit or tuxedo, taking into account the formality of the wedding and the overall wedding style. Coordinate with the bride's attire and choose colours that complement the wedding theme.

5. **Bridesmaid and Groomsmen Attire: ** Work with your wedding party to choose attire that fits your vision and colour scheme. Consider the preferences and body types of your attendants while making decisions.

6. **Consider the Season: ** Keep the weather and season in mind when selecting attire. Choose lighter fabrics for warm weather and warmer fabrics for cooler temperatures.

7. **Venue and Theme: ** The wedding venue and theme should influence your attire choices. Ensure that your outfits align with the overall ambiance of the wedding.

8. **Alterations and Tailoring: ** Schedule fittings and alterations with a professional seamstress or tailor to ensure the perfect fit for all wedding attire.

9. **Comfort Matters: ** Prioritize comfort in your attire choices, as you'll be wearing them for an extended period. Consider the length of the dress or the height of heels for ease of movement.

10. **Cultural and Family Traditions: ** If you have cultural or family traditions related to wedding attire, incorporate them into your choices to honour your heritage.

11. **Hair and Makeup: ** Plan hair and makeup trials before the wedding day to finalize the look you want. Ensure that your wedding party is also comfortable with their chosen hairstyles and makeup.

12. **Grooming for Groom and Groomsmen: ** Discuss grooming preferences with the groom and groomsmen. Decide whether you want them to have a uniform look or allow individual styles within certain guidelines.

13. **Backup Attire: ** Have a backup plan in case of any unexpected mishaps with attire on the wedding day. Keep emergency sewing kits and accessories on hand.

14. **Dress Code for Guests:** Clearly communicate the dress code for guests on your wedding invitations or wedding website. This will help them dress appropriately for your big day.

15. **Feel Confident and Beautiful:** On the wedding day, focus on feeling confident and beautiful in your chosen attire. Remember that this is a celebration of love, and your happiness will shine through your appearance.

Finding the perfect attire for your wedding day and coordinating the outfits of your wedding party will contribute to the overall aesthetics and ambiance of your celebration. By planning ahead and considering the preferences of all involved, you'll create a cohesive and stylish look that will be remembered for years to come.

Chapter 8: Designing a Picture-Perfect Setting: Décor and Theme Development

Creating a picture-perfect setting for your wedding involves thoughtfully designing the décor and developing a cohesive theme. This chapter will guide you through the process of transforming your venue into a stunning and personalized space that reflects your vision and style.

1. **Refine Your Theme: ** Revisit the theme and style you defined earlier in your wedding planning process. Whether it's rustic, bohemian, classic, modern, or a fusion of styles, use it as the foundation for your décor decisions.

2. **Colour Palette: ** Choose a colour palette that complements your wedding theme and overall vision. Consider the season, venue, and the emotions you want the colours to evoke.

3. **Centrepieces and Table Settings: ** Work with your florist and decorator to design beautiful centrepieces that align with your theme and colour scheme. Select table linens, napkins, and dinnerware that enhance the overall table setting.

4. **Ceremony Décor:** Create a captivating atmosphere for your ceremony. Decorate the aisle with flowers or candles and consider an eye-catching backdrop for exchanging vows.

5. **Lighting:** Lighting plays a significant role in setting the mood for your wedding. Incorporate candles, fairy lights, string lights, or unique fixtures to create a romantic and magical ambiance.

6. **Personal Touches:** Infuse your personalities and love story into the décor. Include sentimental items, photos, or customized elements that are meaningful to you as a couple.

7. **Signage and Stationery:** Design and display signage that guides your guests and adds to the overall aesthetic. This includes welcome signs, seating charts, and table numbers. Coordinate your stationery with your theme as well.

8. **Outdoor Décor:** If your wedding is outdoors, make the most of the natural surroundings. Enhance the beauty of the landscape with minimalistic decorations that complement the environment.

9. **Indoor Décor:** Transform indoor spaces with drapery, flower installations, and creative use of props. Utilize the venue's architecture to your advantage.

10. **Creative Installations:** Consider unique installations like hanging florals, arches, or chandeliers to make a statement and create a focal point.

11. **Sweetheart Table or Head Table:** Design a special table for you and your partner that stands out from the rest. Add personalized touches to make it feel truly yours.

12. **Guest Favors and Gifts:** Select thoughtful guest Favors that tie into your theme. These can double as decor pieces at each place setting.

13. **Interactive Elements:** Incorporate interactive elements like photo booths, guest books, or DIY stations for a memorable and engaging experience.

14. **Lounge Areas:** Create cozy lounge areas for guests to relax and mingle. Use comfortable seating, cushions, and soft furnishings to make it invite.

15. **Professional Help: ** Consider hiring a wedding decorator or stylist who can bring your vision to life and take care of all the details. Their expertise will ensure a polished and cohesive look.

Remember, the key to designing a picture-perfect setting is consistency and attention to detail. Every element should work together harmoniously to create an ambiance that captivates and delights both you and your guests. With careful planning and creativity, your wedding décor will be an expression of your love story and an unforgettable experience for everyone in attendance.

Chapter 9: Culinary Delights: Menu Planning and Catering

A memorable wedding includes delightful culinary experiences for you and your guests. Menu planning and selecting the right caterer are essential to ensure that your wedding feast is a feast to remember. This chapter will guide you through the process of crafting a delectable menu and finding the perfect catering team.

1. **Discuss Preferences and Dietary Restrictions: ** Sit down with your partner to discuss your culinary preferences and any dietary restrictions you or your guests may have. Consider both of your favourite foods and cuisines.

2. **Define Your Culinary Style: ** Determine the style of cuisine you want to serve, whether it's formal plated meals, buffet, family-style, or food stations. Ensure it complements your wedding theme and atmosphere.

3. **Venue Restrictions and Amenities: ** Check with your venue regarding any restrictions on outside catering or specific facilities available for food preparation.

4. **Research Caterers:** Start researching reputable caterers in your area. Read reviews, request quotes, and compare their offerings.

5. **Tastings and Menu Selection:** Schedule tastings with your top caterers to sample their dishes. Narrow down the menu options and select dishes that excite your taste buds.

6. **Consider Seasonal and Local Ingredients:** opt for seasonal and locally sourced ingredients for a fresh and sustainable menu. Discuss this preference with your caterer.

7. **Appetizers and Hors d'oeuvres:** Select a variety of appetizers and hors d'oeuvres to keep guests satisfied during cocktail hour.

8. **Entrees and Side Dishes:** Choose a diverse range of entrees and side dishes to cater to different tastes and dietary preferences. Include options for vegetarians, vegans, and those with allergies.

9. **Beverage Selection:** Discuss the beverage options, including alcoholic and non-alcoholic beverages, with your caterer or a separate bartender.

10. **Interactive Food Stations:** Consider incorporating interactive food stations, such as a pasta bar, taco station, or dessert display. This adds a fun and engaging element to the dining experience.

11. **Cake and Desserts:** Select your wedding cake design and flavours. Additionally, consider offering a variety of desserts to satisfy guests' sweet cravings.

12. **Presentation and Styling:** Discuss the presentation and styling of the food with your caterer. Elegant presentation enhances the overall dining experience.

13. **Service and Staff:** Inquire about the number of staff provided by the caterer and their level of expertise in serving at weddings.

14. **Budget Considerations: ** Be transparent about your budget with the caterer and work together to create a menu that fits within your financial plan.

15. **Final Confirmation and Details: ** Confirm the finalized menu, service details, and logistics with your caterer closer to the wedding date. Ensure they have all necessary information about the event timeline.

Remember that the culinary experience is an integral part of your wedding celebration. A well-crafted menu and attentive catering team will leave a lasting impression on your guests and make your wedding truly unforgettable. Collaborate with your caterer to create a culinary journey that reflects your love and tastes, and delights everyone in attendance.

Chapter 10: A Sweet Soundtrack: Music and Entertainment

Music and entertainment play a significant role in setting the tone and atmosphere of your wedding celebration. This chapter will guide you through the process of selecting the perfect soundtrack and entertainment to create a joyful and memorable experience for you and your guests.

1. **Define Your Music Style: ** Determine the musical style that resonates with you and your partner. Whether it's classical, jazz, pop, rock, country, or a mix of genres, choose music that reflects your personalities and love story.

2. **Ceremony Music: ** Select music for different parts of the ceremony, such as the processional, recessional, and any special moments during the ceremony. Consider live musicians, such as a string quartet or a solo vocalist.

3. **Reception Entertainment: ** Decide on the type of entertainment you want for the reception. Options include a live band, DJ, or a combination of both. Choose one that will keep the dance floor alive, and your guests engaged.

4. **Book Early:** Top musicians and entertainers get booked quickly, so secure your preferred choices as early as possible.

5. **Live Performances:** If you opt for live entertainment, attend live performances by the band or musicians you're considering. This will give you a better sense of their style and how they engage with the audience.

6. **Set the Mood:** Work with your chosen musicians or DJ to create a playlist that sets the right mood for each part of the wedding, from the cocktail hour to the last dance.

7. **First Dance Song:** Choose a meaningful song for your first dance as a married couple. It should be a song that holds special significance to your relationship.

8. **Guest Requests:** If your entertainment allows for it, consider offering a guest request list. This way, your guests can feel involved in the music selection.

9. **Plan for Special Performances:** If you or your guests have any special musical talents, plan for surprise performances or karaoke sessions during the reception.

10. **Consider Other Entertainment:** Explore additional entertainment options, such as photo booths, games, or cultural performances, to keep guests entertained throughout the event.

11. **Audiovisual Setup:** Ensure that your chosen venue has the necessary audiovisual equipment for your entertainment needs.

12. **Timeline and Coordination:** Coordinate with your musicians or DJ to create a timeline for the reception, including announcements, speeches, and specific musical highlights.

13. **Special Dedications:** Consider dedicating certain songs to important people in your life during the reception, such as parents, grandparents, or close friends.

14. **Plan for Lasting Memories:** opt for a memorable grand exit with a sparkler send-off or a special song to close the night.

15. **Review Contracts: ** Before finalizing agreements, carefully review contracts with your chosen musicians or entertainment professionals to ensure all terms are clear.

The right music and entertainment will elevate the joy and celebration of your wedding day. A thoughtfully curated playlist and engaging performances will leave a lasting impression on you and your guests, creating beautiful memories that you'll cherish for a lifetime.

Chapter 11: Invitation Etiquette: Stationery and Guest Communication

Invitations and guest communication set the tone for your wedding and provide essential information to your guests. This chapter will guide you through invitation etiquette, from designing the perfect stationery to effectively communicating with your guests.

1. **Start Early: ** Begin working on your wedding invitations and stationery well in advance. This allows you enough time for design, printing, and addressing.

2. **Design and Theme: ** Create a cohesive design for your wedding stationery that aligns with your chosen theme and colours. Carry the design across save-the-date cards, invitations, and other stationery.

3. **Invitation Wording: ** Choose appropriate and clear wording for your invitations. Include essential details such as the date, time, venue, RSVP information, and any dress code.

4. **Save-the-Date Cards:** Send out save-the-date cards six to eight months before the wedding to give guests ample time to plan and make arrangements.

5. **Invitation Suites:** Consider a complete invitation suite that includes the main invitation, RSVP card, accommodations card, and any other necessary information.

6. **Print Quality:** Invest in high-quality printing for your invitations and stationery to ensure they look elegant and professional.

7. **Guest List Management:** Keep your guest list organized and up to date. Use a spreadsheet or guest management tool to track RSVPs and dietary preferences.

8. **Addressing Invitations:** Address your invitations with proper etiquette. Include titles and full names of recipients, and use calligraphy or elegant fonts for a sophisticated touch.

9. **RSVP Deadline:** Set a reasonable RSVP deadline that allows you enough time to finalize your guest count with vendors.

10. **Response Cards:** Include response cards with stamped envelopes to make it easy for guests to RSVP.

11. **Digital RSVPs:** Consider offering a digital RSVP option for guests who prefer to respond online.

12. **Welcome Packets:** For destination weddings, provide welcome packets with additional information about the location, nearby activities, and a schedule of wedding events.

13. **Communicate Itinerary:** Send out an itinerary of wedding events to guests before the wedding day. This ensures they are informed about the schedule and can plan accordingly.

14. **Thank-You Cards:** Plan ahead for thank-you cards. Send them out promptly after the wedding to express gratitude to your guests for their presence and gifts.

15. **Etiquette for Plus-Ones:** Clearly indicate on the invitations if guests are allowed to bring a plus-one, based on your guest list and budget constraints.

Effective invitation etiquette ensures that your guests feel valued and well-informed, leading to a smoother and more enjoyable wedding experience for everyone. Thoughtfully designed stationery and clear communication will set the tone for your wedding celebration and make your guests feel appreciated and excited to be part of your special day.

Chapter 12: Making it Legal: Marriage Licenses and Ceremony Requirements

Before you say, "I do," there are important legal aspects to take care of to ensure your marriage is recognized. This chapter will guide you through obtaining a marriage license and understanding the ceremony requirements to make your union official.

1. **Research Legal Requirements:** Begin by researching the legal requirements for obtaining a marriage license in your country, state, or region. Each location may have different rules and waiting periods.

2. **Marriage License Application:** Visit the appropriate government office or website to apply for a marriage license. Gather all required documents, such as identification, proof of residency, and any necessary paperwork.

3. **Waiting Period:** Some places have a waiting period between obtaining the marriage license and holding the ceremony. Be sure to account for this when planning your wedding date.

4. **Officiant:** Decide who will officiate your wedding ceremony. It can be a religious leader, a judge, a justice of the peace, or someone else legally authorized to perform marriages in your location.

5. **Pre-Marital Counselling:** In some places, pre-marital counselling is required before obtaining a marriage license. Check if this is a requirement in your area and complete any necessary sessions.

6. **Venue and Location Permits:** If you're having a destination wedding or a ceremony at a public venue, check if you need any additional permits or permissions to hold the wedding there.

7. **Legal Witnesses:** Find out how many witnesses are required to sign the marriage certificate and make arrangements for them to be present during the ceremony.

8. **Customizing the Ceremony:** Work with your officiant to customize the wedding ceremony to reflect your beliefs, values, and love story. Include readings, vows, and rituals that are meaningful to you as a couple.

9. **Marriage Certificate Signing:** Ensure that the marriage certificate is signed correctly by you, your partner, the officiant, and the required witnesses immediately after the ceremony.

10. **Name Change Process:** If you plan to change your last name after marriage, research the legal process and requirements for name change in your jurisdiction.

11. **Destination Weddings:** If you're having a destination wedding, research whether your marriage will be recognized in your home country and what additional steps may be required.

12. **Photocopies and Backup Documents:** Make photocopies of all important documents, including the marriage license and certificate, and keep them in a safe place.

13. **Registering Your Marriage:** After the wedding, ensure that your marriage is legally registered with the appropriate government office.

14. **Obtain Certified Copies:** Obtain certified copies of your marriage certificate for legal and administrative purposes, such

as changing identification documents or updating your marital status.

15. **Enjoy Your Marriage Journey: ** Once all the legal formalities are taken care of, relax and enjoy the journey of marriage with your partner, creating beautiful memories together.

Taking care of the legal requirements for your wedding ensures that your marriage is legally recognized and valid. By following the necessary steps and obtaining the proper documentation, you can focus on celebrating your love and embarking on a beautiful journey together as a married couple.

Chapter 13: Moments that Matter: Planning the Ceremony and Vows

The wedding ceremony is the heart of your celebration, where you and your partner publicly declare your love and commitment to each other. This chapter will guide you through planning the ceremony and crafting meaningful vows for a truly heartfelt and unforgettable moment.

1. **Reflect on Your Relationship:** Take time to reflect on your relationship and what marriage means to both of you. Consider the values and promises you want to include in your ceremony.

2. **Choose Ceremonial Elements:** Decide on any ceremonial elements you want to include, such as unity candle lighting, handfasting, sand ceremony, or a cultural ritual that holds significance for you.

3. **Consult with Your Officiant:** Work closely with your officiant to discuss the structure and flow of the ceremony. Collaborate on creating a ceremony that represents your love story and personalities.

4. **Welcome and Introductions:** Begin the ceremony with a warm welcome to your guests and a brief introduction to your relationship.

5. **Readings and Quotes:** Select readings or quotes that resonate with you as a couple. These can be religious, spiritual, or secular passages that convey the emotions you wish to express.

6. **Personalize Your Vows:** Write personalized vows that express your love, promises, and commitments to each other. Be sincere, heartfelt, and true to yourselves.

7. **Practice Your Vows:** Practice reciting your vows beforehand to feel comfortable and confident during the ceremony.

8. **Incorporate Music:** Select meaningful music to accompany different parts of the ceremony, such as the processional, recessional, and any special moments during the ceremony.

9. **Include Loved Ones:** Honor important family members or friends during the ceremony, whether through readings, songs, or symbolic gestures.

10. **Moment of Silence:** Include a moment of silence to remember loved ones who are no longer with you or to reflect on the journey that led you to this moment.

11. **Exchange of Rings:** Prepare heartfelt words to accompany the exchange of rings, symbolizing your commitment and unity.

12. **Share Your Love Story:** Consider having your officiant share snippets of your love story, how you met, and your journey together, adding a personal touch to the ceremony.

13. **Create a Keepsake Program:** Design a keepsake program that outlines the ceremony order and includes the readings and music selections.

14. **Practice the Processional:** Rehearse the processional with your wedding party to ensure a smooth and coordinated entrance.

15. **Embrace the Moment:** On the day of the ceremony, take a deep breath, embrace the moment, and immerse yourself in the love and emotions of the occasion.

Your wedding ceremony and vows are an opportunity to declare your love and commitment in front of those closest to you. By planning a heartfelt and meaningful ceremony, you'll create cherished memories that will stay with you and your guests forever. Embrace the significance of the moment and savour every second as you begin this new chapter in your lives together.

Chapter 14: Celebrating in Style: Reception Planning and Traditions

The wedding reception is a joyful celebration where you and your guests come together to mark the beginning of your married life. This chapter will guide you through reception planning and introduce some classic and meaningful wedding traditions.

1. **Reception Venue: ** Choose a reception venue that complements your wedding theme and can comfortably accommodate your guest count. Consider indoor and outdoor spaces based on the season and weather.

2. **Seating Arrangements: ** Plan the seating arrangements carefully to ensure that guests feel comfortable and can easily interact with one another.

3. **Reception Timeline: ** Work with your wedding planner or coordinator to create a reception timeline that includes key moments, such as the grand entrance, dinner service, toasts, and the first dance.

4. **Grand Entrance:** Make a grand entrance to the reception as a newly married couple. Consider adding special effects like confetti or fog for a dramatic touch.

5. **Welcome Speech:** Begin the reception with a heartfelt welcome speech to express your gratitude to everyone for being part of your special day.

6. **Dinner Menu:** Finalize the dinner menu with your caterer, ensuring that it caters to various dietary preferences and provides a delightful culinary experience.

7. **Toasts and Speeches:** Allocate time for toasts and speeches from family and friends. Encourage speakers to keep their speeches concise and heartfelt.

8. **First Dance:** Share your first dance as a married couple. Practice beforehand or take dance lessons to make the moment even more special.

9. **Parent Dances:** Plan dances with your parents or those who have played a significant role in your life.

10. **Cutting the Cake:** Perform the cake-cutting ceremony together, symbolizing your first shared task as a married couple.

11. **Bouquet and Garter Toss:** Decide if you want to include the bouquet toss and garter toss traditions in your reception.

12. **Dancing and Entertainment:** Ensure the dance floor is set up for a night of celebration. Keep the energy high with music that appeals to various age groups and tastes.

13. **Photography and Videography:** Work with your photographers and videographers to capture the precious moments of the reception.

14. **Guest Book and Photo Booth:** Set up a guest book for guests to leave well wishes and a photo booth for fun, candid snapshots.

15. **Last Dance and Send-Off:** Plan a memorable last dance and consider a send-off with sparklers or confetti as you head into your new life together.

Wedding traditions are an opportunity to add depth and meaning to your celebration. However, feel free to customize and include traditions that hold significance to you and your partner. Ultimately, the reception is a time to celebrate your love and the start of your journey together with the people who matter most to you.

Chapter 15: From Bachelorette to Honeymoon: Pre-Wedding Events and Post-Wedding Bliss

The period surrounding your wedding is filled with special events and cherished moments. This chapter will guide you through pre-wedding events, such as bachelorette parties and rehearsal dinners, as well as the post-wedding bliss of your honeymoon.

1. **Bachelorette Party:** Coordinate with your maid of honour or bridesmaids to plan a bachelorette party that suits your preferences. Whether it's a night out on the town or a relaxing weekend getaway, make it a memorable celebration with your closest friends.

2. **Bachelor Party:** If your partner is having a bachelor party, encourage open communication about the plans to ensure everyone is comfortable with the arrangements.

3. **Rehearsal Dinner:** Plan a rehearsal dinner the night before the wedding, inviting immediate family members, wedding party, and other key participants. It's a time to relax and share in the excitement before the big day.

4. **Post-Wedding Brunch:** Consider hosting a post-wedding brunch for close family and friends. It's an opportunity to express your gratitude and spend quality time with loved ones.

5. **Thank-You Gifts:** Prepare thoughtful thank-you gifts for your wedding party and anyone who contributed to making your wedding special.

6. **Pack for the Honeymoon:** Before the wedding, ensure that you've packed everything you'll need for the honeymoon. Double-check travel documents, passports, and any other essentials.

7. **Honeymoon Planning:** Plan your honeymoon itinerary together, considering both relaxation and exciting activities to create a well-rounded experience.

8. **Inform Vendors:** Inform your wedding vendors about your honeymoon dates to avoid any potential scheduling conflicts.

9. **Honeymoon Budget:** Set a budget for your honeymoon and plan activities and accommodations accordingly.

10. **Inform Guests:** If you'll be leaving for your honeymoon immediately after the wedding, inform your guests during the reception so they can plan their goodbyes accordingly.

11. **Wedding Dress and Suit Care:** Arrange for the proper cleaning and preservation of your wedding attire after the celebration.

12. **Send Thank-You Cards:** Once you return from your honeymoon, send out thank-you cards promptly to show appreciation for the love and support you received.

13. **Relax and Unwind:** On your honeymoon, take time to relax and unwind, cherishing the moments of solitude and quality time with your partner.

14. **Capture Honeymoon Memories:** Take photos and videos during your honeymoon to capture the beautiful memories you'll cherish for a lifetime.

15. **Celebrate Your New Journey:** Celebrate the start of your married life together, savouring each moment of post-wedding bliss and the excitement of your shared future.

The time surrounding your wedding is filled with love, joy, and anticipation. Embrace the special events leading up to the wedding day and enjoy the honeymoon as a chance to create unforgettable memories with your partner. Remember to take care of each other and relish in the joy of beginning your new journey together as a married couple.

Chapter 16: Tackling Logistics: Transportation, Accommodations, and Guest Management

Effective logistics are essential for a smooth and enjoyable wedding experience for both you and your guests. This chapter will guide you through managing transportation, accommodations, and guest logistics to ensure everyone feels comfortable and well taken care of during your wedding celebration.

1. **Transportation Coordination: ** Arrange transportation for you, your wedding party, and guests between venues, especially if there are multiple locations for the ceremony, reception, and accommodations.

2. **Guest Accommodations: ** Reserve room blocks at nearby hotels or accommodation options for your out-of-town guests. Negotiate group rates to help your guests with their bookings.

3. **Welcome Packages: ** Consider creating welcome packages for guests staying at hotels. Include helpful information about the area, a schedule of wedding events, and any thoughtful amenities.

4. **Transport to Ceremony Venue:** Arrange transportation for you and your wedding party to the ceremony venue, ensuring everyone arrives on time.

5. **Guest Arrival Assistance:** Arrange for greeters or signage at the ceremony and reception venues to help guests find their way and feel welcomed.

6. **Parking Solutions:** Provide clear information about parking options for guests, including valet services or nearby parking facilities.

7. **Local Recommendations:** Offer guests a list of nearby attractions, restaurants, and activities to enjoy during their free time.

8. **RSVP Tracking:** Keep track of RSVPs and meal preferences using a spreadsheet or online tool to provide accurate numbers to your vendors.

9. **Seating Assignments:** Organize seating arrangements thoughtfully and communicate them to your guests in advance, either through a seating chart or place cards.

10. **Communication with Guests:** Stay in touch with your guests throughout the planning process, sending reminders and updates as needed.

11. **Childcare Arrangements:** If you're having an adults-only wedding, help guests with childcare arrangements and suggest local babysitting services.

12. **Special Needs Accommodations:** Inquire about any special accommodations your guests may require, such as wheelchair accessibility or dietary restrictions.

13. **Emergency Contact Information:** Collect emergency contact information from your guests in case you need to reach them during the wedding events.

14. **Timeline Communication:** Provide your wedding party and important guests with a detailed timeline of events to ensure everyone is on the same page.

15. **Thank-You for Attendance:** Show your appreciation to your guests for traveling and attending your wedding with a heartfelt thank-you message or small token of appreciation.

By attending to logistics with care and consideration, you'll make your wedding celebration comfortable and enjoyable for everyone involved. Clear communication and thoughtful planning ensure that your guests can relax and fully enjoy the special moments of your wedding day. Taking care of the logistical details allows you and your partner to focus on the love and joy of your wedding celebration.

Chapter 17: Staying Stress-Free: Organization and Time Management Tips

Planning a wedding can be overwhelming, but staying organized and managing your time effectively can help reduce stress and ensure a smooth planning process. This chapter will provide you with practical tips to stay organized and manage your time efficiently throughout your wedding journey.

1. **Create a Wedding Planning Timeline:** Develop a detailed timeline that outlines all the tasks, deadlines, and milestones from the engagement to the wedding day.

2. **Use a Wedding Planning Checklist:** Utilize a comprehensive checklist that covers all aspects of wedding planning, from venue selection to honeymoon arrangements.

3. **Set Priorities:** Identify the most critical tasks and prioritize them. Focus on essential elements first and then move on to smaller details.

4. **Break Down Tasks:** Divide larger tasks into smaller, manageable sub-tasks. This will make the process less overwhelming and more achievable.

5. **Stay Organized with Folders and Binders:** Keep all wedding-related documents, contracts, and inspiration materials organized in labelled folders or binders.

6. **Use Technology:** Explore wedding planning apps and tools to help you stay organized, set reminders, and track your progress.

7. **Delegate Responsibilities:** Enlist the help of trusted friends, family members, or a wedding planner to share the workload and ensure tasks are handled efficiently.

8. **Schedule Regular Planning Meetings:** If you have a wedding planner or team helping you, schedule regular meetings to discuss progress, upcoming tasks, and any adjustments needed.

9. **Allocate Time for Wedding Planning:** Set aside dedicated time each week for wedding planning. Treat it as an appointment to ensure progress is made consistently.

10. **Avoid Procrastination:** Don't put off tasks. Tackle them promptly to prevent last-minute rushes and reduce stress.

11. **Maintain Communication:** Keep open lines of communication with all involved parties to ensure everyone is on the same page.

12. **Take Breaks:** Give yourself breaks from wedding planning to recharge. Engage in activities that help you relax and de-stress.

13. **Practice Self-Care:** Prioritize self-care during the planning process. Get enough rest, eat well, and engage in activities that bring you joy.

14. **Stay Flexible:** Be prepared for unexpected changes and adapt accordingly. Flexibility will help you handle any challenges that may arise.

15. **Celebrate Milestones:** Acknowledge and celebrate the completion of major tasks or reaching significant milestones in your wedding planning journey.

Remember that wedding planning should be an enjoyable experience, not just a checklist of tasks. By staying organized, managing your time effectively, and keeping a positive mindset, you can navigate the planning process with ease and create the wedding of your dreams. Take one step at a time, savour the journey, and look forward to a beautiful and memorable wedding celebration.

Chapter 18: Navigating Wedding Etiquette: Dos and Don'ts for a Smooth Celebration

Wedding etiquette plays a crucial role in ensuring a harmonious and respectful wedding celebration. This chapter will guide you through the dos and don'ts of wedding etiquette, helping you navigate potential challenges and create a positive experience for all involved.

Dos:

1. **Do Be Thoughtful with Invitations:** Send out invitations on time, clearly indicating the RSVP deadline and any other necessary information.

2. **Do Address Invitations Properly:** Address invitations with correct titles and full names. Use calligraphy or elegant fonts for a sophisticated touch.

3. **Do Send Thank-You Notes:** Express gratitude with personalized thank-you notes for gifts, attendance, and any help received during the wedding planning process.

4. **Do Consider Plus-Ones:** Thoughtfully decide on plus-ones based on your guest list and budget, and clearly indicate on invitations if guests are allowed to bring a guest.

5. **Do Communicate Clearly:** Keep guests informed of any changes to the schedule or arrangements and provide directions and contact information if necessary.

6. **Do Be Respectful of Traditions:** If you or your partner come from different cultural or religious backgrounds, be respectful of each other's traditions and incorporate them thoughtfully into the celebration.

7. **Do Thank Your Wedding Party:** Show appreciation to your wedding party with meaningful gifts and acknowledge their support and effort.

8. **Do Be Gracious:** Be gracious and understanding if some guests cannot attend the wedding due to personal reasons or conflicts.

Don'ts:

1. **Don't Make Last-Minute Changes:** Avoid making significant changes to the guest list, seating arrangements, or the wedding schedule at the eleventh hour.

2. **Don't Overshare on social media:** Refrain from posting every detail of the wedding planning process on social media. Save the major announcements and updates for your invitations and personal communications.

3. **Don't Micromanage Vendors:** Trust your chosen vendors to do their jobs well. Micromanaging can cause unnecessary stress for both you and the vendors.

4. **Don't Assume Plus-Ones:** Don't assume that all single guests want to bring a plus-one. Clearly indicate on the invitation if a guest is allowed to bring a date.

5. **Don't Exclude Family Members:** Be sensitive to family dynamics and avoid excluding important family members from wedding events without valid reasons.

6. **Don't Discuss Costs with Guests:** Avoid discussing the cost of the wedding with guests. It is a private matter between you and your partner.

7. **Don't Forget to Say Hello:** Make an effort to greet and thank all your guests during the wedding reception, even if it's just a brief acknowledgment.

By following wedding etiquette, you will create an atmosphere of respect, appreciation, and love throughout your celebration. Thoughtful communication, graciousness, and adherence to tradition will make your wedding a positive and memorable experience for everyone involved. Remember, good etiquette sets the tone for a smooth and harmonious wedding celebration.

Chapter 19: Handling Wedding-Day Emergencies: Troubleshooting and Crisis Management

While we hope for a smooth and flawless wedding day, unexpected challenges can arise. Being prepared to handle emergencies with grace and composure is essential. This chapter will guide you through troubleshooting and crisis management to help you navigate any unforeseen situations on your special day.

1. **Create a Wedding-Day Emergency Kit:** Prepare an emergency kit with essential items like safety pins, a sewing kit, stain remover, pain relievers, band-aids, tissues, and other useful supplies.

2. **Appoint a Point of Contact:** Designate a trusted friend, family member, or wedding planner as the point of contact for vendors and guests. They can handle any issues that may arise, allowing you to focus on enjoying your day.

3. **Weather Contingency Plan:** If you're having an outdoor wedding, have a clear weather contingency plan in place. Be prepared to move the ceremony or reception indoors if needed.

4. **Vendor Communication:** Ensure that all vendors have the necessary contact information for your designated point of contact and each other, so they can coordinate if required.

5. **Stay Calm and Flexible:** If something doesn't go as planned, stay calm and flexible. Your composure will set the tone for how others manage the situation.

6. **Guest Safety:** Prioritize guest safety. If there is any potential danger, take quick action to ensure everyone's well-being.

7. **Keep Guests Informed:** If there are any changes to the schedule or arrangements, communicate promptly with guests to avoid confusion.

8. **Backup Equipment:** Have backup equipment available for critical elements like sound systems, microphones, and cameras.

9. **First Aid Plan:** Know the location of the nearest first-aid station or medical facility and have someone capable of administering basic first aid if needed.

10. **Lost Items:** If a guest or vendor misplaces something valuable, be proactive in assisting them in locating it.

11. **Vendor Disruptions:** In case of a vendor no-show or delay, have a backup plan in place or a list of alternative vendors to contact.

12. **Power Outages:** If there's a power outage, have battery-powered lights or lanterns on hand, and inform guests of any safety measures.

13. **Deal with Disagreements Gracefully:** If conflicts arise between guests or family members, handle them discreetly and diplomatically.

14. **Take Care of Yourself:** Stay hydrated, eat well, and take breaks when needed. It is essential to take care of yourself during a long and eventful day.

15. **Remember the Big Picture:** Amidst any emergencies, remember the big picture: the celebration of your love and the

commitment you're making to your partner. Focus on the joy and significance of the day.

Handling wedding-day emergencies with grace and efficiency will help you overcome challenges and still enjoy your wedding day to the fullest. By having contingency plans in place and being prepared to address unexpected situations, you can navigate any crises that may arise, creating lasting memories of a beautiful and resilient celebration.

Chapter 20: The Big Day Arrives: Enjoying Every Moment of Your Wedding

The day you have been eagerly anticipating has finally arrived—your wedding day! This chapter will guide you on how to savour and cherish every moment of this special occasion as you celebrate your love and commitment to each other.

1. **Begin with a Calm Morning:** Start your day with a relaxed and peaceful morning. Consider practicing yoga, meditating, or enjoying a quiet breakfast with loved ones.

2. **Get Ready with Your Bridal Party:** Share the excitement and laughter with your bridal party as you all get ready together. Capture candid moments with your photographer to treasure forever.

3. **Stay Present and Mindful:** Throughout the day, stay present and mindful. Take moments to soak in the joy and emotions, knowing that this day is about you and your partner.

4. **Take First-Look Photos:** Consider having a first-look photo session with your partner before the ceremony. This

intimate moment allows you to share your love privately before the celebration begins.

5. **Exchange Personal Notes: ** Write heartfelt notes to each other and exchange them before the ceremony. These personal messages will become cherished keepsakes.

6. **Have a Quiet Moment Together: ** Find a few moments alone with your partner during the day. It is an opportunity to connect amidst the whirlwind of activities.

7. **Engage with Guests: ** Take time to interact with your guests during the reception. Express gratitude for their presence and make lasting memories with them.

8. **Dance Like Nobody's Watching: ** Let loose on the dance floor and enjoy the celebration with your loved ones. Dance with joy and abandon, celebrating your love together.

9. **Capture Candid Moments: ** Allow your photographer and videographer to capture candid moments of you and your guests, as these often become the most cherished memories.

10. **Enjoy the Food: ** Savor the delicious food and drinks you've selected for the reception. Take time to eat and hydrate throughout the day to stay energized.

11. **Take Breaks as Needed: ** If you feel overwhelmed, take short breaks to collect yourself and refresh.

12. **Embrace Imperfections: ** Accept that not everything may go exactly as planned, and that's okay. Embrace imperfections and remember that what matters most is the love you share.

13. **Celebrate with a Last Dance: ** Close the night with a last dance, surrounded by your loved ones. Take in the moment before your grand exit.

14. **End on a High Note: ** If you have a grand exit planned, end the night on a high note with sparklers, confetti, or other celebratory elements.

15. **Stay in the Moment: ** As the day comes to an end, cherish the memories you've created. Remember that your love story continues, and the best is yet to come.

Your wedding day is a celebration of your love, surrounded by the people who mean the most to you. By staying present, embracing the emotions, and enjoying every moment, you will create a cherished memory that will forever hold a special place in your hearts. Treasure the love and joy that surround you on this remarkable day, and let it be the foundation of a beautiful and fulfilling journey together as a married couple. Congratulations and best wishes for a lifetime of happiness!

Below is a wedding planning checklist tailored for planning a wedding in the United Kingdom. Keep in mind that this is a general guide, and you can customize it based on your specific preferences and needs:

12-24 Months Before the Wedding:

☐ Set a budget and discuss financial contributions with family members if applicable.

☐ Choose your wedding date and have backup options in case of venue availability.

☐ Create a guest list and finalize the number of guests.

☐ Book your ceremony and reception venues.

☐ Hire a wedding planner or coordinator if desired.

☐ Begin researching and booking key vendors:

- Photographer

- Videographer

- Car Hire

- Florist

- Caterer

- Entertainment (band/DJ)

- Wedding officiant

- Cake baker

- Hair and makeup artist

☐ Start looking for wedding attire and accessories.

☐ Arrange wedding-day transportation for you and your guests if needed.

☐ Send save-the-date cards to out-of-town guests.

8-10 Months Before the Wedding:

☐ Choose and order your wedding attire, including any accessories.

☐ Finalize the guest list and collect RSVPs.

☐ Start planning your honeymoon and book flights and accommodations.

☐ Order wedding stationery, including invitations, RSVP cards, and thank-you cards.

☐ Plan the wedding ceremony and select readings, vows, and any cultural or religious elements.

☐ Book accommodations for out-of-town guests.

☐ Attend pre-marital counselling if required or desired.

6-8 Months Before the Wedding:

☐ Book any remaining vendors:

   - Transportation for the wedding day

   - Lighting and decor rentals

   - Photo booth

☐ Choose and order wedding rings.

☐ Schedule dress fittings and alterations.

☐ Plan the menu and schedule a tasting with the caterer.

☐ Arrange for any necessary legal paperwork, such as marriage licenses.

4-6 Months Before the Wedding:

☐ Send out wedding invitations.

☐ Plan and book accommodations for the wedding night.

☐ Organize bridesmaids' and groomsmen's attire.

☐ Finalize ceremony details with the officiant.

☐ Plan the order of events for the reception, including speeches and toasts.

2-4 Months Before the Wedding:

☐ Finalize the menu and provide a final guest count to the caterer.

☐ Confirm all vendor bookings and details.

☐ Create a wedding-day timeline and share it with vendors and the wedding party.

☐ Purchase wedding favours and gifts for the wedding party.

☐ Attend dress fittings and make any final adjustments.

☐ Confirm transportation arrangements for the wedding day.

1-2 Months Before the Wedding:

☐ Follow up with guests who have not RSVPed.

☐ Have a final meeting with the venue and caterer to confirm details.

☐ Write and practice your vows if you're having personalized vows.

☐ Confirm the order of events with the DJ or band.

☐ Create a seating chart for the reception.

1-2 Weeks Before the Wedding:

☐ Confirm all final details with vendors.

☐ Prepare final payments and tips for vendors.

☐ Pack for the honeymoon.

☐ Have a final dress fitting and arrange for pickup or delivery.

☐ Give final guest numbers to the venue and caterer.

On the Wedding Day:

☐ Enjoy your wedding day and cherish every moment!

☐ Have fun with your guests and celebrate your love together.

After the Wedding:

☐ Send thank-you notes to guests and vendors.

☐ Arrange for the preservation of your wedding dress if desired.

☐ Review and select photos from the photographer and videographer.

☐ Change your name and update legal documents if applicable.

Remember that wedding planning can be overwhelming at times, so don't hesitate to ask for help from friends, family, or a wedding planner. Stay organized, stay flexible, and most importantly,

enjoy the journey to your special day! And Congratulations!

Printed in Great Britain
by Amazon